D1346362

to ....

from ....

THE NATION'S
FAVOURITE
LOVE POEMS

The 10 most popular poems from the 1997 poll
to find the nation's favourite love poem.

1. Sonnet from the Portuguese XLIII How do I love thee?
Let me count the ways
ELIZABETH BARRETT BROWNING

*

2. He Wishes for the Cloths of Heaven
W. B. YEATS

3. Twelve Songs IX Stop all the clocks, cut off the telephone
W. H. AUDEN

4. A Red, Red Rose
ROBERT BURNS

5. Sonnet 116 Let me not to the marriage of true minds
WILLIAM SHAKESPEARE

6. To His Coy Mistress
ANDREW MARVELL

7. Sonnet 18 Shall I compare thee to a summer's day?
WILLIAM SHAKESPEARE

8. Remember
CHRISTINA G. ROSSETTI

9. Renouncement
ALICE MEYNELL

10. When you are Old
W. B. YEATS

*

THE NATION'S
FAVOURITE
LOVE POEMS

— ◇ —

Ana Catarina de Neiva
BBC Worldwide
Int. Publishing
80. Woodlane   BBC BOOKS
London.
W12.0TT.

Also available from B B C Books:

THE NATION'S FAVOURITE POEMS
ISBN: 0 563 38782 3

An audio cassette to accompany the above book
is produced by B B C Radio Collection.
ZBBC1889
ISBN: 0 563 38987 7

Published by BBC Books,
an imprint of BBC Worldwide Limited,
Woodlands,
80 Wood Lane,
London W12 0TT

First published 1997
This hardback edition first published 1998
Compilation © BBC Books 1997
Poems © individual copyright holders

ISBN 0 563 38432 8

Set in Stempel Garamond by Ace Filmsetting Ltd, Frome.
Printed in Great Britain by Martins the Printers Ltd,
Berwick Upon Tweed
Bound in Great Britain by Hunter and Foulis Ltd, Edinburgh
Cover printed by Belmont Press, Northampton.

CONTENTS

— ⬦ —

– Celebration and Adoration –

– Love in Absence –

– Love Fulfilled –

– *In Warning of Love* –

– *Love Lost and Love Remembered* –

INTRODUCTION

— ⬦ —

I n 1995, *The Bookworm* asked BBC viewers and listeners to vote for their favourite poems. The result was a clear win for 'If' by Rudyard Kipling. In 1996 we held a vote to discover the nation's favourite modern poem and again a clear winner emerged almost at once: Jenny Joseph's hymn to growing old disgracefully, 'Warning'. It was a popular win with everyone except the poet herself, who feels that her other work has been neglected as a result of the huge popularity of 'Warning':

> When I am an old woman I shall wear purple
> With a red hat which doesn't go, and doesn't suit me.

One of the surprises about the top twenty in both years was how few love poems made it into the charts. Surprising because, according to a recent survey, we are most prone to reading and even writing poetry when we're in love. People who gleefully abandoned poetry when they left school, begin to see the point of 'How do I love thee? Let me count the ways', or a passionate Shakespeare sonnet, when they find themselves in the grip of love. Many couples who marry in church include love poems in the service and poetry rivals gin as consolation for the broken-hearted: poetry is cheaper than gin.

So this year we want to find out which love poems have really touched the nation's heart. To help you choose we have compiled a selection of the love poems that have been most anthologized and requested on television and radio. Also included are the poems most often read at weddings ('Sonnet from the Portuguese XIV' and Kahlil Gibran's 'On Marriage' from *The Prophet* are the most popular). We have even asked poets themselves for their favourites (a special thank you to Wendy Cope for suggesting Edwin Muir's wonderful 'The Confirmation'). The result is a glorious confection of extravagant delights – proof, if anyone needed it, that beneath its sensible outer garments Britain is a nation of romance junkies.

Whatever your symptoms this book has the cure! If you've just met the love of your life then turn immediately to the Love's Beginnings section and administer daily doses of Wendy Cope's 'After the Lunch'. If you're in such a fever of excitement that you crave something stronger, try 'The Canonization' by John Donne, or the erotic fan dance of John Fuller's 'Valentine'. And for the poetic equivalent of a post-coital cigarette there is Auden's bittersweet 'Lullaby', that begins:

> Lay your sleeping head, my love,
> Human on my faithless arm.

If you are getting married, this book contains a whole congregation of poems that will bring tears to the eyes of the bride's mother: 'Wedding Wind' by Philip Larkin makes a change from Shakespeare, or if solemnity is not your style then what about 'The Owl and the Pussy-Cat', surely the most charming whirlwind romance in verse!

> They dined on mince, and slices of quince
> Which they ate with a runcible spoon;
> And hand in hand, on the edge of the sand
> They danced by the light of the moon.

It might be wise to skip the In Warning of Love section if you've already booked the hall and ordered the dress. Poems such as 'La Belle Dame Sans Merci' or Ted Hughes' feral 'Lovesong' are very much the morning after the night before. And if it's too late and your lover has gone, then take consolation in the fact that all the big guns have been there too. In fact, there are many more poems about lost love than about love fulfilled. Maybe they are just a miserable bunch, or perhaps the depths are easier to write about than the heights, but poets seem to thrive on heartbreak. Thomas Hardy, who features heavily in this section, detested his first wife Emma, but when she died he produced some of the most heart-rending poems of lost love ever written.

If it's comfort you're looking for then be warned – the outlook is bleak. For most poets there is no respite from the pain of loss, 'Time does not bring relief; you all have lied,' is Edna St.Vincent Millay's harsh take on getting over it. Of course, they come to terms with it eventually, but no self-respecting poet is going to let the past go without squeezing it dry.

This book is an attempt to collect together everyone's favourite love poems, old, new, happy, sad, erotic or wistful. If you've ever had the experience of being in love and suddenly finding lines from poems filling your head unbidden and you need to track them down, then I hope you'll find them in this book. The only category that is completely missing is love songs. There are strong arguments for including 'We Can Work it Out' by Lennon and McCartney or 'Night and Day' by Cole Porter, but judging by your response to last year's invitation to include lyrics among your favourite modern poems, not many of you consider them poems. John Lennon's 'Imagine' was the highest placed lyric coming in at number 22.

Enjoy this book alone or in company. And wherever you've got to in the tunnel of love, remember that some poet has been there before you.

DAISY GOODWIN

Love's Beginnings

— ◇ —

ELIZABETH BARRETT BROWNING 1806–61

SONNET FROM THE PORTUGUESE XIV

If thou must love me, let it be for nought
Except for love's sake only. Do not say
'I love her for her smile . . her look . . her way
Of speaking gently, . . for a trick of thought
That falls in well with mine, and certes brought
A sense of pleasant ease on such a day' –
For these things in themselves, Beloved, may
Be changed, or change for thee, – and love, so wrought,
May be unwrought so. Neither love me for
Thine own dear pity's wiping my cheeks dry,
Since one might well forget to weep who bore
Thy comfort long, and lose thy love thereby.
But love me for love's sake, that evermore
Thou may'st love on through love's eternity.

JOHN CLARE 1793–1864

FIRST LOVE

I ne'er was struck before that hour
    With love so sudden and so sweet
Her face it bloomed like a sweet flower
    And stole my heart away complete
My face turned pale a deadly pale
    My legs refused to walk away
And when she looked what could I ail
My life and all seemed turned to clay

And then my blood rushed to my face
    And took my eyesight quite away
The trees and bushes round the place
    Seemed midnight at noon day
I could not see a single thing
    Words from my eyes did start
They spoke as chords do from the string
    And blood burnt round my heart

Are flowers the winters choice
    Is love's bed always snow
She seemed to hear my silent voice
    Not loves appeals to know
I never saw so sweet a face
    As that I stood before
My heart has left its dwelling place
    And can return no more –

W. B. YEATS 1865–1939

HE WISHES FOR THE CLOTHS OF HEAVEN

Had I the heavens' embroidered cloths,
Enwrought with golden and silver light,
The blue and the dim and the dark cloths
Of night and light and the half-light,
I would spread the cloths under your feet:
But I, being poor, have only my dreams;
I have spread my dreams under your feet;
Tread softly because you tread on my dreams.

W.H. AUDEN 1907–73

OH TELL ME THE TRUTH ABOUT LOVE

Some say that love's a little boy,
    And some say it's a bird,
Some say it makes the world go round,
    And some say that's absurd,
And when I asked the man next-door,
    Who looked as if he knew,
His wife got very cross indeed,
    And said it wouldn't do.

    Does it look like a pair of pyjamas,
      Or the ham in a temperance hotel?
    Does it odour remind one of llamas,
      Or has it a comforting smell?
    Is it prickly to touch as a hedge is,
      Or soft as eiderdown fluff?
    Is it sharp or quite smooth at the edges?
      O tell me the truth about love.

Our history books refer to it
    In cryptic little notes,
It's quite a common topic on
    The Transatlantic boats;
I've found the subject mentioned in
    Accounts of suicides,
And even seen it scribbled on
    The backs of railway-guides.

    Does it howl like a hungry Alsation,
      Or boom like a military band?
    Could one give a first-rate imitation
      On a saw or a Steinway Grand?
    Is its singing at parties a riot?
      Does it only like Classical stuff?
    Will it stop when one wants to be quiet?
      O tell me the truth about love.

I looked inside the summer-house;
    It wasn't ever there:
I tried the Thames at Maidenhead,
    And Brighton's bracing air.
I don't know what the blackbird sang,
    Or what the tulip said;
But it wasn't in the chicken-run,
    Or underneath the bed.

    Can it pull extraordinary faces?
      Is it usually sick on a swing?
    Does it spend all its time at the races,
      Or fiddling with pieces of string?
    Has it views of its own about money?
      Does it think Patriotism enough?
    Are its stories vulgar but funny?
      O tell me the truth about love.

When it comes, will it come without warning
    Just as I'm picking my nose?
Will it knock on my door in the morning,
    Or tread in the bus on my toes?
Will it come like a change in the weather?
    Will its greeting be courteous or rough?
Will it alter my life altogether?
    O tell me the truth about love.

January 1938

ROBERT HERRICK 1591–1674

DELIGHT IN DISORDER

A sweet disorder in the dresse
Kindles in cloathes a wantonnesse:
A Lawne about the shoulders thrown
Into a fine distraction: –
An erring Lace, which here and there
Enthralls the Crimson Stomacher: –
A Cuffe neglectfull, and thereby
Ribbands to flow confusedly: –
A winning wave (deserving Note)
In the tempestuous petticote: –
A carelesse shoe-string, in whose tye
I see a wilde civility: –
Doe more bewitch me, than when Art
Is too precise in every part.

EDMUND SPENSER 1552–99

SONNET LXXV

One day I wrote her name vpon the strand,
  but came the waues and washed it away:
  agayne I wrote it with a second hand,
  but came the tyde, and made my paynes his pray.
Vayne man, sayd she, that doest in vaine assay,
  a mortall thing so to immortalize,
  for I my selue shall lyke to this decay,
  and eek my name bee wyped out lykewize.
Not so, (quod I) let baser things deuize
  to dy in dust, but you shall liue by fame:
  my verse your vertues rare shall eternize,
  and in the heuens wryte your glorious name.
Where whenas death shall all the world subdew,
  our loue shall liue, and later life renew.

ALFRED, LORD TENNYSON 1809–92

COME INTO THE GARDEN MAUD
from *Maud*

I

Come into the garden, Maud,
  For the black bat, night, has flown,
Come into the garden, Maud,
  I am here at the gate alone;
And the woodbine spices are wafted abroad,
  And the musk of the rose is blown.

II

For a breeze of morning moves,
  And the planet of Love is on high,
Beginning to faint in the light that she loves
  On a bed of daffodil sky,
To faint in the light of the sun she loves,
  To faint in his light, and to die.

WENDY COPE 1945–

AFTER THE LUNCH

On Waterloo Bridge, where we said our goodbyes,
The weather conditions bring tears to my eyes.
I wipe them away with a black woolly glove
And try not to notice I've fallen in love.

On Waterloo Bridge I am trying to think:
This is nothing. You're high on the charm and the drink.
But the juke-box inside me is playing a song
That says something different. And when was it wrong?

On Waterloo Bridge with the wind in my hair
I am tempted to skip. *You're a fool.* I don't care.
The head does its best but the heart is the boss –
I admit it before I am halfway across.

ALFRED, LORD TENNYSON 1809–92

NOW SLEEPS THE CRIMSON PETAL
from *The Princess*

'Now sleeps the crimson petal, now the white;
Nor waves the cypress in the palace walk;
Nor winks the gold fin in the porphyry font.
The firefly wakens: waken thou with me.

'Now droops the milk-white peacock like a ghost,
And like a ghost she glimmers on to me.

'Now lies the Earth all Danaë to the stars,
And all thy heart lies open unto me.

'Now slides the silent meteor on, and leaves
A shining furrow, as thy thoughts in me.

'Now folds the lily all her sweetness up,
And slips into the bosom of the lake.
So fold thyself, my dearest, thou, and slip
Into my bosom and be lost in me.'

BENJAMIN JONSON 1572–1637

TO CELIA

Drinke to me, onely, with thine eyes,
    And I will pledge with mine;
Or leave a kisse but in the cup,
    And I'll not look for wine.
The thirst that from the soule doth rise,
    Doth aske a drink divine:
But might I of Jove's *Nectar* sup,
    I would not change for thine.
I sent thee, late, a rosie wreath,
    Not so much honoring thee,
As giving it a hope, that there
    It could not withered bee.
But thou thereon did'st onely breath,
    And sent'st it backe to me:
Since when it growes, and smells, I sweare,
    Not of it selfe, but thee.

JOHN DONNE 1572–1631

THE BAITE

Come live with mee, and bee my love,
And wee will some new pleasures prove
Of golden sands, and christall brookes,
With silken lines, and silver hookes.

There will the river whispering runne
Warm'd by thy eyes, more than the Sunne.
And there the'inamor'd fish will stay,
Begging themselves they may betray.

When thou wilt swimme in that live bath,
Each fish, which every channell hath,
Will amorously to thee swimme,
Gladder to catch thee, than thou him.

If thou, to be so seene, beest loath,
By Sunne, or Moone, thou darknest both,
And if my selfe have leave to see,
I need not their light, having thee.

Let others freeze with angling reeds,
And cut their legges, with shells and weeds,
Or treacherously poore fish beset,
With strangling snare, or windowie net:

Let coarse bold hands, from slimy nest
The bedded fish in banks out-wrest,
Or curious traitors, sleavesilke flies
Bewitch poore fishes wandring eyes.

For thee, thou needst no such deceit,
For thou thy selfe art thine owne bait;
That fish, that is not catch'd thereby,
Alas, is wiser farre than I.

PERCY BYSSHE SHELLEY 1792–1822

LOVE'S PHILOSOPHY

The fountains mingle with the river
And the rivers with the ocean,
The winds of heaven mix for ever
With a sweet emotion;
Nothing in the world is single,
All things by a law divine
In one another's being mingle –
Why not I with thine?

See the mountain's kiss high heaven
And the waves clasp one another;
No sister-flower would be forgiven
If it disdain'd its brother:

And the sunlight clasps the earth,
And the moonbeams kiss the sea –
What are all these kissings worth,
If thou kiss not me?

WENDY COPE 1945–

VALENTINE

My heart has made its mind up
And I'm afraid it's you.
Whatever you've got lined up,
My heart has made its mind up
And if you can't be signed up
This year, next year will do.
My heart has made its mind up
And I'm afraid it's you.

CHRISTOPHER MARLOWE 1564–93

THE PASSIONATE SHEPHERD TO HIS LOVE

Come live with me and be my Love,
And we will all the pleasures prove
That hills and valleys, dale and field,
And all the craggy mountains yield.

There will we sit upon the rocks
And see the shepherds feed their flocks,
By shallow rivers, to whose falls
Melodious birds sing madrigals.

There will I make thee beds of roses
And a thousand fragrant posies,
A cap of flowers, and a kirtle
Embroider'd all with leaves of myrtle.

A gown made of the finest wool,
Which from our pretty lambs we pull,
Fair linèd slippers for the cold,
With buckles of the purest gold.

A belt of straw and ivy buds
With coral clasps and amber studs:
And if these pleasures may thee move,
Come live with me and be my Love.

Thy silver dishes for thy meat
As precious as the gods do eat,
Shall on an ivory table be
Prepared each day for thee and me.

The shepherd swains shall dance and sing
For thy delight each May-morning:
If these delights thy mind may move,
Then live with me and be my Love.

SIR JOHN BETJEMAN 1906–84

A SUBALTERN'S LOVE-SONG

Miss J. Hunter Dunn, Miss J. Hunter Dunn,
Furnish'd and burnish'd by Aldershot sun,
What strenuous singles we played after tea,
We in the tournament – you against me!

Love-thirty, love-forty, oh! weakness of joy,
The speed of a swallow, the grace of a boy,
With carefullest carelessness, gaily you won,
I am weak from your loveliness, Joan Hunter Dunn.

Miss Joan Hunter Dunn, Miss Joan Hunter Dunn,
How mad I am, sad I am, glad that you won.
The warm-handled racket is back in its press,
But my shock-headed victor, she loves me no less.

Her father's euonymus shines as we walk,
And swing past the summer-house, buried in talk,
And cool the verandah that welcomes us in
To the six-o'clock news and a lime-juice and gin.

The scent of the conifers, sound of the bath,
The view from my bedroom of moss-dappled path,
As I struggle with double-end evening tie,
For we dance at the Golf Club, my victor and I.

On the floor of her bedroom lie blazer and shorts
And the cream-coloured walls are be-trophied with sports,
And westering, questioning settles the sun
On your low-leaded window, Miss Joan Hunter Dunn.

The Hillman is waiting, the light's in the hall,
The pictures of Egypt are bright on the wall,
My sweet, I am standing beside the oak stair
And there on the landing's the light on your hair.

By roads 'not adopted,' by woodlanded ways,
She drove to the club in the late summer haze,
Into nine-o'clock Camberley, heavy with bells
And mushroomy, pine-woody, evergreen smells.

Miss Joan Hunter Dunn, Miss Joan Hunter Dunn,
I can hear from the car-park the dance has begun.
Oh! full Surrey twilight! importunate band!
Oh! strongly adorable tennis-girl's hand!

Around us are Rovers and Austins afar,
Above us, the intimate roof of the car,
And here on my right is the girl of my choice,
With the tilt of her nose and the chime of her voice,

And the scent of her wrap, and the words never said,
And the ominous, ominous dancing ahead.
We sat in the car park till twenty to one
And now I'm engaged to Miss Joan Hunter Dunn.

EDWARD FITZGERALD 1809–83

from THE RUBAIYAT OF OMAR KHAYYAM

A Book of Verses underneath the Bough,
A Jug of Wine, a Loaf of Bread – and Thou
   Beside me singing in the Wilderness –
O, Wilderness were Paradise enow!

Some for the Glories of This World; and some
Sigh for the Prophet's Paradise to come;
   Ah, take the Cash, and let the Credit go,
Nor heed the rumble of a distant Drum!

Look to the blowing Rose about us – 'Lo,
Laughing,' she says, 'into the world I blow.
   At once the silken tassel of my Purse
Tear, and its Treasure on the Garden throw.'

And those who husbanded the Golden Grain
And those who flung it to the winds like Rain,
   Alike to no such aureate Earth are turned
As, buried once, Men want dug up again.

The Worldly Hope men set their Hearts upon
Turn Ashes – or it prospers; and anon,
   Like Snow upon the Desert's dusty Face,
Lighting a little hour or two – is gone.

Think, in this battered Caravanserai
Whose Portals are alternate Night and Day,
   How Sultan after Sultan with his Pomp
Abode his destined Hour, and went his way.

They say the Lion and the Lizard keep
The Courts where Jamshyd gloried and drank deep:
   And Bahram, that great Hunter – the wild Ass
Stamps o'er his Head, but cannot break his Sleep.

I sometimes think that never blows so red
The Rose as where some buried Caesar bled;
   That every Hyacinth the Garden wears
Dropt in her Lap from some once lovely Head.

And this reviving Herb whose tender Green
Fledges the River-Lip on which we lean –
   Ah, lean upon it lightly! for who knows
From what once lovely Lip it springs unseen!

Ah, my Beloved, fill the Cup that clears
TO-DAY of past Regrets and future Fears:
   To-morrow! – Why, To-morrow I may be
Myself with Yesterday's Seven thousand Years.

For some we loved, the loveliest and the best
That from his Vintage rolling Time hath prest,
   Have drunk their Cup a Round or two before,
And one by one crept silently to rest.

And we, that now make merry in the Room
They left, and Summer dresses in new bloom,
   Ourselves must we beneath the Couch of Earth
Descent – ourselves to make a Couch – for whom?

Ah, make the most of what we yet may spend,
Before we too into the Dust descend;
   Dust into Dust, and under Dust to lie,
Sans Wine, sans Song, sans Singer, and – sans End!

JOHN DONNE 1572–1631

THE FLEA

Marke but this flea, and marke in this,
How little that which thou deny'st me is;
Mee it suck'd first, and now sucks thee,
And in this flea, our two bloods mingled bee;
Confesse it, this cannot be said
A sinne, or shame, or losse of maidenhead,
      Yet this enjoyes before it wooe,
      And pamper'd swells with one blood made of two,
      And this, alas, is more than wee would doe.

Oh stay, three lives in one flea spare,
Where wee almost, nay more than maryed are:
This flea is you and I, and this
Our marriage bed, and marriage temple is;
Though parents grudge, and you, w'are met,
And cloysterd in these living walls of Jet.
      Though use make thee apt to kill mee,
      Let not to this, selfe murder added bee,
      And sacrilege, three sinnes in killing three.

Cruell and sodaine, hast thou since
Purpled thy naile, in blood of innocence?
In what could this flea guilty bee,
Except in that drop which it suckt from thee?
Yet thou triumph'st, and saist that thou
Find'st not thy selfe, nor mee the weaker now;
      'Tis true, then learne how false, feares bee;
      Just so much honor, when thou yeeld'st to mee,
      Will wast, as this flea's death tooke life from thee.

ROBERT HERRICK 1591–1674

TO THE VIRGINS, TO MAKE MUCH OF TIME

Gather ye Rose-buds while ye may,
  Old Time is still a flying:
And this same flower that smiles to day,
  Tomorrow will be dying.

The glorious Lamp of Heaven, the Sun,
  The higher he's a getting;
The sooner will his Race be run,
  And nearer he's to Setting.

That Age is best, which is the first,
  When Youth and Blood are warmer;
But being spent, the worse, and worst
  Times, still succeed the former.

Then be not coy, but use your time;
  And while ye may, go marry:
For having lost but once your prime,
  You may for ever tarry.

ANDREW MARVELL 1621–78

TO HIS COY MISTRESS

Had we but world enough, and time,
This coyness, Lady, were no crime
We would sit down and think which way
To walk and pass our long love's day.
Thou by the Indian Ganges' side
Should'st rubies find: I by the tide
Of Humber would complain. I would
Love you ten years before the Flood,
And you should, if you please, refuse
Till the conversion of the Jews.
My vegetable love should grow
Vaster than empires, and more slow.
An hundred years should go to praise
Thine eyes and on thy forehead gaze;
Two hundred to adore each breast,
But thirty thousand to the rest.
An age at least to every part,
And the last age should show your heart.
For, Lady, you deserve this state,
Nor would I love at lower rate.

    But at my back I always hear
Time's wingèd chariot hurrying near;
And yonder all before us lie
Deserts of vast eternity.
Thy beauty shall no more be found,
Nor, in my marble vault, shall sound
My echoing song: then worms shall try
That long preserved virginity,
And your quaint honour turn to dust,
And into ashes all my lust.
The grave's a fine and private place,
But none, I think, do there embrace.

Now therefore, while the youthful hue
Sits on thy skin like morning dew,
And while thy willing soul transpires
At every pore with instant fires,
Now let us sport us while we may,
And now, like amorous birds of prey,
Rather at once our time devour
Than languish in his slow-chapt power.
Let us roll all our strength and all
Our sweetness up into one ball,
And tear our pleasures with rough strife
Through the iron gates of life:
Thus, though we cannot make our sun
Stand still, yet we will make him run.

JOHN DONNE 1572–1631

THE CANONIZATION

For God's sake hold your tongue, and let me love,
    Or chide my palsy, or my gout,
My five grey hairs, or ruined fortune flout,
    With wealth your state, your mind with arts improve,
        Take you a course, get you a place,
        Observe his Honour, or his Grace,
Or the King's real, or his stamped face
    Contemplate; what you will, approve,
    So you will let me love.

Alas, alas, who's injured by my love?
    What merchant's ships have my sighs drowned?
Who says my tears have overflowed his ground?
    When did my colds a forward spring remove?
        When did the heats which my veins fill
        Add one more to the plaguy bill?
Soldiers find wars, and lawyers find out still
    Litigious men, which quarrels move,
    Though she and I do love.

Call us what you will, we are made such by love;
    Call her one, me another fly,
We are tapers too, and at our own cost die,
    And we in us find the eagle and the dove,
        The phoenix riddle hath more wit
        By us; we two being one, are it.
So to one neutral thing both sexes fit
    We die and rise the same, and prove
    Mysterious by this love.

We can die by it, if not live by love,
  And if unfit for tombs and hearse
Our legend be, it will be fit for verse;
  And if no piece of chronicle we prove,
    We'll build in sonnets pretty rooms;
    As well a well wrought urn becomes
The greatest ashes, as half-acre tombs,
  And by these hymns, all shall approve
  Us canonized for love:

And thus invoke us; 'You whom reverend love
  Made one another's hermitage;
You, to whom love was peace, that now is rage;
  Who did the whole world's soul contract, and drove
    Into the glasses of your eyes
    (So made such mirrors, and such spies,
That they did all to you epitomize,)
  Countries, towns, courts: beg from above
  A pattern of your love!'

EDMUND WALLER 1606–87

SONG

Goe lovely Rose,
Tell her that wasts her time and mee,
That now shee knowes,
When I resemble her to thee,
How sweet and fayr shee seems to bee.

Tell her that's young,
And shuns to have her graces spide,
That hadst thou sprung
In deserts where no men abide,
Thou must have uncommended dy'd.

Small is the worth
Of beauty from the light retir'd;
Bid her come forth,
Suffer her selfe to bee desir'd,
And not blush so to be admir'd.

Then dye, that shee
The common fate of all things rare
May read in thee:
How small a part of time they share,
That are so wondrous sweet and faire.

WENDY COPE 1945–

GIVING UP SMOKING

There's not a Shakespeare sonnet
Or a Beethoven quartet
That's easier to like than you
Or harder to forget.

You think that sounds extravagant?
I haven't finished yet –
I like you more than I would like
To have a cigarette.

Celebration and Adoration

— ✧ —

WILLIAM SHAKESPEARE 1564–1616

SONNET 18

Shall I compare thee to a summer's day?
Thou art more lovely and more temperate:
Rough winds do shake the darling buds of May,
And summer's lease hath all too short a date:
Sometime too hot the eye of heaven shines,
And often is his gold complexion dimm'd,
And every fair from fair sometime declines,
By chance or natures changing course untrimm'd:
But thy eternal summer shall not fade,
Nor lose possession of that fair thou owest,
Nor shall death brag thou wandrest in his shade,
When in eternal lines to time thou growest,
    So long as men can breathe or eyes can see
    So long lives this, and this gives life to thee.

JOHN UPDIKE 1932–

DEA EX MACHINA

In brief, shapeliness and smoothness of the flesh are desirable
because they are signs of biological efficiency.

David Angus, *The New York Times Book Review*

My love is like Mies van der Rohe's
    'Machine for living'; she,
Divested of her underclothes,
    Suggests efficiency.

Her supple shoulders call to mind
    A set of bevelled gears;
Her lower jaw has been aligned
    To hinge behind her ears.

Her hips, sweet ball-and-socket joints,
    Are padded to perfection;
Each knee, with its patella, points
    In just the right direction.

Her fingertips remind me of
    A digital computer;
She couldn't be, my well-tooled love,
    A millimeter cuter.

GEORGE GORDON, LORD BYRON 1788–1824

SHE WALKS IN BEAUTY

She walks in beauty, like the night
  Of cloudless climes and starry skies;
And all that's best of dark and bright
  Meet in her aspect and her eyes:
Thus mellow'd to that tender light
  Which heaven to gaudy day denies.

One shade the more, one ray the less,
  Had half impair'd the nameless grace
Which waves in every raven tress,
  Or softly lightens o'er her face;
Where thoughts serenely sweet express
  How pure, how dear their dwelling-place.

And on that cheek, and o'er that brow,
  So soft, so calm, yet eloquent,
The smiles that win, the tints that glow,
  But tell of days in goodness spent,
A mind at peace with all below,
  A heart whose love is innocent!

WENDY COPE 1945–

FLOWERS

Some men never think of it.
You did. You'd come along
And say you'd nearly brought me flowers
But something had gone wrong.

The shop was closed. Or you had doubts –
The sort that minds like ours
Dream up incessantly. You thought
I might not want your flowers.

It made me smile and hug you then.
Now I can only smile.
But, Look, the flowers you nearly brought
Have lasted all this while.

WILLIAM SHAKESPEARE 1564–1616

SONNET 29

When in disgrace with fortune and men's eyes
   I all alone beweep my outcast state,
And trouble deaf heaven with my bootless cries,
   And look upon myself, and curse my fate,
Wishing me like to one more rich in hope,
   Featured like him, like him with friends possessed,
Desiring this man's art, and that man's scope,
   With what I most enjoy contented least;
Yet in these thoughts myself almost despising,
   Haply I think on thee, and then my state,
Like to the lark at break of day arising
   From sullen earth, sings hymns at heaven's gate;
      For thy sweet love remembered such wealth brings
      That then I scorn to change my state with kings.

SEAMUS HEANEY 1939–

FIELD WORK

I

Where the sally tree went pale in every breeze,
where the perfect eye of the nesting blackbird watched,
where one fern was always green

I was standing watching you
take the pad from the gatehouse at the crossing
and reach to lift a white wash off the whins.

I could see the vaccination mark
stretched on your upper arm, and smell the coal smell
of the train that comes between us, a slow goods,

waggon after waggon full of big-eyed cattle.

II

But your vaccination mark is on your thigh,
an O that's healed into the bark.

Except a dryad's not a woman
you are my wounded dryad

in a mothering smell of wet
and ring-wormed chestnuts.

Our moon was small and far,
was a coin long gazed at

brilliant on the *Pequod's* mast
across Atlantic and Pacific waters.

III

Not the mud slick,
not the black weedy water
full of alder cones and pock-marked leaves.

Not the cow parsley in winter
with its old whitened shins and wrists,
its sibilance, its shaking.

Not even the tart green shade of summer
thick with butterflies
and fungus plump as a leather saddle.

No. But in a still corner,
braced to its pebble-dashed wall,
heavy, earth-drawn, all mouth and eye,

the sunflower, dreaming umber.

IV

Catspiss smell,
the pink bloom open:
I press a leaf
of the flowering currant
on the back of your hand
for the tight slow burn
of its sticky juice
to prime your skin,
and your veins to be crossed
criss-cross with leaf-veins.
I lick my thumb
and dip it in mould,
I anoint the anointed
leaf-shape. Mould
blooms and pigments
the back of your hand
like a birthmark –
my umber one,
you are stained, stained
to perfection.

CAROL ANN DUFFY 1955–

WARMING HER PEARLS

Next to my own skin, her pearls. My mistress
bids me wear them, warm them, until evening
when I'll brush her hair. At six, I place them
round her cool, white throat. All day I think of her,

resting in the Yellow room, contemplating silk
or taffeta, which gown tonight? She fans herself
whilst I work willingly, my slow heat entering
each pearl. Slack on my neck, her rope.

She's beautiful. I dream about her
in my attic bed; picture her dancing
with tall men, puzzled by my faint persistent scent
beneath her French perfume, her milky stones.

I dust her shoulders with a rabbit's foot,
watch the soft blush seep through her skin
like an indolent sigh. In her looking-glass
my red lips part as though I want to speak.

Full moon. Her carriage brings her home. I see
her every movement in my head . . . Undressing,
taking off her jewels, her slim hand reaching
for the case, slipping naked into bed, the way

she always does . . . And I lie here awake,
knowing the pearls are cooling even now
in the room where my mistress sleeps. All night
I feel their absence and I burn.

WILLIAM SHAKESPEARE 1564–1616

SONNET 106

When in the chronicle of wasted time
I see descriptions of the fairest wights,
And beauty making beautiful old rime
In praise of ladies dead and lovely knights,
Then, in the blazon of sweet beauty's best,
Of hand, of foot, of lip, of eye, of brow,
I see their antique pen would have exprest
Even such a beauty as you master now.
So all their praises are but prophecies
Of this our time, all you prefiguring;
And, for they lookt but with divining eyes,
They had not skill enough your worth to sing:
    For we, which now behold these present days,
    Have eyes to wonder, but lack tongues to praise.

SYLVIA PLATH 1932–63

YOU'RE

Clownlike, happiest on your hands,
Feet to the stars, and moon-skulled,
Gilled like a fish. A Common-sense
Thumbs-down on the dodo's mode.
Wrapped up in yourself like a spool,
Trawling your dark as owls do.
Mute as a turnip from the Fourth
Of July to All Fool's Day,
O high-riser, my little loaf.

Vague as fog and looked for like mail.
Farther off than Australia.
Bent-backed Atlas, our travelled prawn.
Snug as a bud and at home
Like a sprat in a pickle jug.
A creel of eels, all ripples.
Jumpy as a Mexican bean.
Right, like a well-done sum.
A clean slate, with your own face on.

CHRISTOPHER MARLOWE 1564–93

THE FACE THAT LAUNCHED A THOUSAND SHIPS
from *Doctor Faustus*

(Doctor Faustus Speaks)

Was this the face that launched a thousand ships?
And burnt the topless towers of Ilium?
Sweet Helen, make me immortal with a kiss:
Her lips suck forth my soul, see where it flies!
Come Helen, come, give me my soul again.
Here will I dwell, for heaven is in these lips,
And all is dross that is not Helena.
I will be Paris, and for love of thee,
Instead of Troy shall Wertenberg be sack'd;
And I will combat with weak Menelaus,
And wear thy colours on my plumed crest;
Yea I will wound Achillis in the heel,
And then return to Helen for a kiss.
O thou art fairer than the evening air,
Clad in the beauty of a thousand stars:
Brighter art thou than flaming Jupiter,
When he appear'd to hapless Semele;
More lovely than the monarch of the sky
In wanton Arethusa's azur'd arms;
And none but thou shalt be my paramour.

JOHN FULLER 1937–

VALENTINE

The things about you I appreciate
    May seem indelicate:
I'd like to find you in the shower
And chase the soap for half an hour.
I'd like to have you in my power
    And see your eyes dilate.
I'd like to have your back to scour
And other parts to lubricate.
Sometimes I feel it is my fate
To chase you screaming up a tower
    Or make you cower
By asking you to differentiate
    Nietzsche from Schopenhauer.
I'd like successfully to guess your weight
    And win you at a fête.
I'd like to offer you a flower.

I like the hair upon your shoulders,
Falling like water over boulders.
I like the shoulders, too: they are essential.
Your collar-bones have great potential
(I'd like all your particulars in folders
    Marked *Confidential*).

I like your cheeks, I like your nose,
I like the way your lips disclose
The neat arrangement of your teeth
(Half above and half beneath)
    In rows.

I like your eyes, I like their fringes.
The way they focus on me gives me twinges.
Your upper arms drive me berserk.
I like the way your elbows work,
    On hinges.

I like your wrists, I like your glands,
I like the fingers on your hands.
I'd like to teach them how to count,
And certain things we might exchange,
Something familiar for something strange.
I'd like to give you just the right amount
     And get some change.

I like it when you tilt your cheek up.
I like the way you nod and hold a teacup.
I like your legs when you unwind them.
Even in trousers I don't mind them.
I like each softly-moulded kneecap.
I like the little crease behind them.
I'd always know, without a recap,
     Where to find them.

I like the sculpture of your ears.
I like the way your profile disappears
Whenever you decide to turn and face me.
I'd like to cross two hemispheres
     And have you chase me.
I'd like to smuggle you across frontiers
Or sail with you at night into Tangiers.
     I'd like you to embrace me.

I'd like to see you ironing your skirt
     And cancelling other dates.
I'd like to button up your shirt.
I like the way your chest inflates.
I'd like to soothe you when you're hurt
Or frightened senseless by invertebrates.

I'd like you even if you were malign
And had a yen for sudden homicide.
I'd let you put insecticide
    Into my wine.
I'd even like you if you were the Bride of Frankenstein
Or something ghoulish out of Mamoulian's *Jekyll and Hyde.*
I'd even like you as my Julian
Of Norwich or Cathleen ni Houlihan.
    How melodramatic
If you were something muttering in attics
Like Mrs Rochester or a student of Boolean mathematics

You are the end of self-abuse.
You are the eternal feminine.
I'd like to find a good excuse
To call on you and find you in.
I'd like to put my hand beneath your chin.
    And see you grin.
I'd like to taste your Charlotte Russe,
I'd like to feel my lips upon your skin,
I'd like to make you reproduce.

I'd like you in my confidence.
I'd like to be your second look.
I'd like to let you try the French Defence
    And mate you with my rook.
I'd like to be your preference
    And hence
I'd like to be around when you unhook.
I'd like to be your only audience,
The final name in your appointment book,
    Your future tense.

EDWIN MUIR 1887–1959

THE CONFIRMATION

Yes, yours, my love, is the right human face.
I in my mind had waited for this long,
Seeing the false and searching for the true,
Then found you as a traveller finds a place
Of welcome suddenly amid the wrong
Valleys and rocks and twisting roads. But you,
What shall I call you? A fountain in a waste,
A well of water in a country dry,
Or anything that's honest and good, an eye
That makes the whole world bright. Your open heart,
Simple with giving, gives the primal deed,
The first good world, the blossom, the blowing seed,
The hearth, the steadfast land, the wandering sea.
Not beautiful or rare in every part.
But like yourself, as they were meant to be.

ADRIAN MITCHELL 1932–

CELIA CELIA

When I am sad and weary
When I think all hope has gone
When I walk along High Holborn
I think of you with nothing on

Love in Absence

— ◇ —

ANON

BOBBY SHAFTO'S GONE TO SEA

Bobby Shafto's gone to sea,
  Silver buckles at his knee;
He'll come back and marry me,
  Bonny Bobby Shafto!

Bobby Shafto's fat and fair,
  Combing down his yellow hair;
He's my love for evermore,
  Bonny Bobby Shafto!

CHRISTINA G. ROSSETTI 1830–94

REMEMBER

Remember me when I am gone away,
  Gone far away into the silent land;
  When you can no more hold me by the hand,
Nor I half turn to go yet turning stay.
Remember me when no more day by day
  You tell me of our future that you plann'd:
  Only remember me; you understand
It will be late to counsel then or pray.
Yet if you should forget me for a while
  And afterwards remember, do not grieve:
  For if the darkness and corruption leave
  A vestige of the thoughts that once I had,
Better by far you should forget and smile
  Than that you should remember and be sad.

CAROL ANN DUFFY 1955–

WORDS, WIDE NIGHT

Somewhere on the other side of this wide night
and the distance between us, I am thinking of you.
The room is turning slowly away from the moon.

This is pleasurable. Or shall I cross that out and say
it is sad? In one of the tenses I singing
an impossible song of desire that you cannot hear.

La lala la. See? I close my eyes and imagine
the dark hills I would have to cross
to reach you. For I am in love with you and this

is what it is like or what it is like in words.

JOHN DONNE 1572–1631

A VALEDICTION : FORBIDDING MOURNING

As virtuous men pass mildly'away,
   And whisper to their soules, to goe,
Whilst some of their sad friends doe say
The breath goes now, and some say, no:

So let us melt, and make no noise,
   No teare-floods, nor sigh-tempests move,
'Twere profanation of our joyes
To tell the layetie our love.

Moving of th'earth brings harmes and feares,
   Men reckon what it did and meant,
But trepidation of the spheares,
   Though greater farre, is innocent.

Dull sublunary lovers love
   (Whose soule is sense) cannot admit
Absence, because it doth remove
   Those things which elemented it.

But we by'a love, so much refin'd,
   That our selves know not what it is,
Inter-assured of the mind,
   Care lesse eyes, lips and hands to misse.

Our two soules therefore, which are one,
   Though I must goe, endure not yet
A breach, but an expansion,
   Like gold to ayery thinnesse beate.

If they be two, they are two so
   As stiffe twin compasses are two,
Thy soule the fixt foot, makes no show
   To move, but doth, if the'other do.

And though it in the center sit,
   Yet when the other far doth rome,
It leanes, and hearkens after it,
   And growes erect, as it comes home.

Such wilt thou be to mee, who must
   Like the'other foot, obliquely runne;
Thy firmnes makes my circle just,
   And makes me end where I begunne.

ROBERT BURNS 1759–1796

A RED, RED ROSE

Tune: *Major Graham*

O my luve's like a red, red rose,
    That's newly sprung in June;
O my luve's like the melodie
    That's sweetly play'd in tune.

As fair art thou, my bonie lass,
    So deep in luve am I,
And I will luve thee still, my Dear,
    Till a' the seas gang dry.

Till a' the seas gang dry, my Dear,
    And the rocks melt wi' the sun:
I will luve thee still, my Dear,
    While the sands o' life shall run.

And fare thee weel, my only Luve,
    And fare thee weel a while!
And I will come again, my Luve,
    Tho' it were ten thousand mile!

RICHARD LOVELACE 1618–58

TO LUCASTA, GOING TO THE WARRES

Tell me not (Sweet) I am unkinde,
   That from the Nunnerie
Of thy chaste breast, and quiet minde,
   To Warre and Armes I flie.

True; A new Mistresse now I chase,
   The first Foe in the Field;
And with a stronger Faith imbrace
   A Sword, a Horse, a Shield.

Yet this Inconstancy is such,
   As you too shall adore;
I could not love thee (Deare) so much,
   Lov'd I not Honour more.

ANON

WESTERN WIND

Western wind, when will thou blow,
  The small rain down can rain?
Christ, if my love were in my arms
  And I in my bed again!

Love Fulfilled

JOHN DONNE 1572–1631

THE GOOD-MORROW

I wonder by my troth, what thou, and I
Did, till we lov'd? were we not wean'd till then?
But suck'd on countrey pleasures, childishly?
Or snorted we i'the seaven sleepers den?
'Twas so; But this, all pleasures fancies bee.
If ever any beauty I did see,
Which I desir'd, and got, t'was but a dreame of thee.

And now good morrow to our waking soules,
Which watch not one another out of feare;
For love, all love of other sights controules,
And makes one little roome, an every where.
Let sea-discoverers to new worlds have gone,
Let Maps to other, worlds on worlds have showne,
Let us possesse one world, each hath one, and is one.

My face in thine eye, thine in mine appeares,
And true plaine hearts doe in the faces rest,
Where can we finde two better hemispheares
Without sharpe North, without declining West?
What ever dyes, was not mixt equally;
If our two loves be one, or, thou and I
Love so alike, that none doe slacken, none can die.

CHRISTINA G. ROSSETTI 1830–94

A BIRTHDAY

My heart is like a singing bird
   Whose nest is in a watered shoot;
My heart is like an apple tree
   Whose boughs are bent with thickset fruit;
My heart is like a rainbow shell
   That paddles in a halcyon sea;
My heart is gladder than all these
   Because my love is come to me.

Raise me a dais of silk and down;
   Hang it with vair and purple dyes;
Carve it in doves and pomegranates
   And peacocks with a hundred eyes;
Work it in gold and silver grapes,
   In leaves and silver fleurs-de-lys;
Because the birthday of my life
   Is come, my love is come to me.

KAHLIL GIBRAN 1883–1931

ON MARRIAGE
from *The Prophet*

Then Almitra spoke again and said, And what of Marriage, master?

And he answered saying:
You were born together, and together you shall be for evermore.
You shall be together when the white wings of death scatter
    your days.
Ay, you shall be together even in the silent memory of God.
But let there be spaces in your togetherness,
And let the winds of the heavens dance between you.

Love one another, but make not a bond of love:
Let it rather be a moving sea between the shores of your souls.
Fill each other's cup but drink not from one cup.
Give one another of your bread but eat not from the same loaf.
Sing and dance together and be joyous, but let each one of
    you be alone.
Even as the strings of a lute are alone though they quiver with
    the same music.

Give your hearts, but not into each other's keeping.
For only the hand of Life can contain your hearts.
And stand together yet not too near together:
For the pillars of the temple stand apart,
And the oak tree and the cypress grow not in each other's
    shadow.

GEORGE HERBERT 1593–1633

LOVE (III)

Love bade me welcome; yet my soul drew back,
    Guilty of dust and sin.
But quick-eyed Love, observing me grow slack
    From my first entrance in,
Drew nearer to me, sweetly questioning
    If I lack'd anything.

'A guest,' I answer'd, 'worthy to be here:'
    Love said, 'You shall be he.'
'I, the unkind, ungrateful? Ah, my dear,
    I cannot look on thee.'
Love took my hand and smiling did reply,
'Who made the eyes but I?'

'Truth, Lord, but I have marr'd them: let my shame
    Go where it doth deserve.'
'And know you not,' says Love, 'Who bore the blame?'
    'My dear, then I will serve.'
'You must sit down,' says Love, 'and taste my meat.'
    So I did sit and eat.

JOHN DONNE 1572–1631

THE UNDERTAKING

I have done one braver thing
   Than all the *Worthies* did,
Yet a braver thence doth spring,
   Which is, to keep that hid.

It were but madness now t'impart
   The skill of specular stone,
When he which can have learn'd the art
   To cut it, can finde none.

So, if I now should utter this,
   Others (because no more
Such stuff to work upon, there is,)
   Would love but as before.

But he who lovelinesse within
   Hath found, all outward loathes,
For he who colour loves, and skinne,
   Loves but their oldest clothes.

If, as I have, you also doe
   Vertue 'attir'd in woman see,
And dare love that, and say so too,
   And forget the Hee and Shee;

And if this love, though placed so,
   From profane men you hide,
Which will no faith on this bestow,
Or, if they doe, deride:

Then you'have done a braver thing
   Than all the *Worthies* did;
And a braver thence will spring,
   Which is, to keepe that hid.

W.H. AUDEN 1907–73

LULLABY

Lay your sleeping head, my love,
Human on my faithless arm;
Time and fevers burn away
Individual beauty from
Thoughtful children, and the grave
Proves the child ephemeral:
But in my arms till break of day
Let the living creature lie,
Mortal, guilty, but to me
The entirely beautiful.

Soul and body have no bounds:
To lovers as they lie upon
Her tolerant enchanted slope
In their ordinary swoon,
Grave the vision Venus sends
Of supernatural sympathy,
Universal love and hope;
While an abstract insight wakes
Among the glaciers and the rocks
The hermit's sensual ecstasy.

Certainty, fidelity
On the stroke of midnight pass
Like vibrations of a bell,
And fashionable madmen raise
Their pedantic boring cry:
Every farthing of the cost,
All the dreaded cards foretell,
Shall be paid, for from this night
Not a whisper, not a thought,
Not a kiss nor look be lost.

Beauty, midnight, vision dies:
Let the winds of dawn that blow
Softly round your dreaming head
Such a day of sweetness show
Eye and knocking heart may bless,
Find the mortal world enough;
Noons of dryness see you fed
By the involuntary powers,
Nights of insult let you pass
Watched by every human love.

WILLIAM SHAKESPEARE 1564–1616

SONNET 116

Let me not to the marriage of true minds
Admit impediments. Love is not love
Which alters when it alteration finds,
Or bends with the remover to remove:
O, no, it is an ever-fixed mark,
That looks on tempests and is never shaken;
It is the star to every wandering bark,
Whose worth's unknown, although his height be taken.
Love's not Time's fool, though rosy lips and cheeks
Within his bending sickle's compass come;
Love alters not with his brief hours and weeks,
But bears it out even to the edge of doom.
  If this be error and upon me proved,
  I never writ, nor no man ever loved.

JOHN DONNE 1572–1631

AIRE AND ANGELS

Twice or thrice had I lov'd thee,
Before I knew thy face or name;
So in a voice, so in a shapelesse flame,
Angells affect us oft, and worship'd bee;
   Still when, to where thou wert, I came,
Some lovely glorious nothing I did see.
   But since my soule, whose child love is,
Takes limmes of flesh, and else could nothing doe.
   More subtile than the parent is,
Love must not be, but take a body too,
    And therefore what thou wert, and who,
      I bid Love aske, and now
That it assume thy body, I allow,
And fixe it selfe in thy lip, eye, and brow.

Whilst thus to ballast love, I thought,
And so more steddily to have gone,
With wares which would sinke admiration,
I saw, I had loves pinnace overfraught,
   Ev'ry thy haire for love to worke upon
Is much too much, some fitter must be sought;
   For, nor in nothing, nor in things
Extreme, and scatt'ring bright, can love inhere;
   Then as an Angell, face, and wings
of aire, not pure as it, yet pure doth weare,
    So thy love may be my loves spheare;
      Just such disparitie
As is twixt Aire and Angells puritie,
'Twixt womens love, and mens will ever bee.

JOHN KEATS 1795–1821

BRIGHT STAR

Bright Star! would I were steadfast as thou art –
Not in lone splendour hung aloft the night,
And watching, with eternal lids apart,
Like Nature's patient sleepless Eremite,
The moving waters at their priestlike task
Of pure ablution round earth's human shores,
Or gazing on the new soft fallen mask
Of snow upon the mountains and the moors –
No – yet still steadfast, still unchangeable,
Pillow'd upon my fair love's ripening breast
To feel for ever its soft fall and swell,
Awake for ever in a sweet unrest;
   Still, still to hear her tender-taken breath,
   And so live ever – or else swoon to death.

JOHN DONNE 1572–1631

THE SUNNE RISING

Busie old foole, unruly Sunne,
Why dost thou thus,
Through windowes, and through curtaines call on us?
Must to thy motions lovers seasons run?
Sawcy pedantique wretch, goe chide
Late schoole boyes, and sowre prentices,
Goe tell Court-huntsmen, that the King will ride,
Call countrey ants to harvest offices;
Love, all alike, no season knowes, nor clyme,
Nor houres, dayes, months, which are the rags of time.

Thy beames, so reverend, and strong
Why shouldst thou thinke?
I could eclipse and cloud them with a winke,
But that I would not lose her sight so long:
If her eyes have not blinded thine,
Looke, and to morrow late, tell mee,
Whether both the'India's of spice and Myne
Be where thou leftst them, or lie here with mee.
Aske for those Kings whom thou saw'st yesterday,
And thou shalt heare, All here in one bed lay.

She'is all States, and all Princes, I,
Nothing else is.
Princes doe but play us; compar'd to this,
All honor's mimique; All wealth alchimie.
Thou sunne art halfe as happy'as wee,
In that the world's contracted thus;
Thine age askes ease, and since thy duties bee
To warme the world, that's done in warming us.
Shine here to us, and thou art every where;
This bed thy center is, these walls, thy spheare.

CHRISTINA G. ROSSETTI 1830–94

THE FIRST DAY

I wish I could remember the first day,
First hour, first moment of your meeting me,
If bright or dim the season, it might be
Summer or Winter for aught I can say.
So unrecorded did it slip away,
So blind was I to see and foresee,
So dull to mark the budding of my tree
That would not blossom yet for many a May.
If only I could recollect it, such
A day of days! I let it come and go
As traceless as a thaw of bygone snow;
It seemed to mean so little, meant so much;
If only now I could recall that touch,
First touch of hand in hand – Did one but know!

SIR JOHN BETJEMAN 1906–84

IN A BATH TEASHOP

'Let us not speak, for the love we bear one another –
 Let us hold hands and look.'
She, such a very ordinary little woman;
 He, such a thumping crook;
But both, for a moment, little lower than the angels
 In the teashop's ingle-nook.

PHILIP LARKIN 1922–85

WEDDING-WIND

The wind blew all my wedding-day,
And my wedding-night was the night of the high wind;
And a stable door was banging, again and again,
That he must go and shut it, leaving me
Stupid in candlelight, hearing rain,
Seeing my face in the twisted candlestick,
Yet seeing nothing. When he came back
He said the horses were restless, and I was sad
That any man or beast that night should lack
The happiness I had.

                Now in the day
All's ravelled under the sun by the wind's blowing.
He has gone to look at the floods, and I
Carry a chipped pail to the chicken-run,
Set it down, and stare. All is the wind
Hunting through clouds and forests, thrashing
My apron and the hanging cloths on the line.
Can it be borne, this bodying-forth by wind
Of joy my actions turn on, like a thread
Carrying beads? Shall I be let to sleep
Now this perpetual morning shares my bed?
Can even death dry up
These new delighted lakes, conclude
Our kneeling as cattle by all-generous waters?

ROBERT BURNS 1759–96

JOHN ANDERSON MY JO

John Anderson my jo, John,
   When we were first acquent;
Your locks were like the raven,
   Your bony brow was brent;
But now your brow is beld, John,
   Your locks are like the snaw;
But blessings on your frosty pow,
   John Anderson my jo.

John Anderson my jo, John,
   We clamb the hill the gither;
And mony a canty day, John,
   We've had wi' ane anither:
Now we maun totter down, John,
   And hand in hand we'll go;
And sleep the gither at the foot,
   John Anderson my jo.

JOHN DONNE 1572–1631

ELEGIE: TO HIS MISTRIS GOING TO BED

Come Madame, come, all rest my powers defie,
Until I labour, I in labour lie.
The foe oft-times having the foe in sight,
Is tir'd with standing though he never fight.
Off with that girdle, like heavens zone glistering,
But a far fairer world encompassing.
Unpin that spangled brest-plate, which you weare
That th'eyes of busy fooles may be stopt there:
Unlace your selfe, for that harmonious chime
Tells me from you that now 'tis your bed time.
Off with that happy buske, which I envye
That still can be, and still can stand so nigh.
Your gownes going off such beauteous state reveales
As when from flowery meades th'hills shadow steales.
Off with your wyrie coronet and showe
The hairy dyadem which on you doth growe.
Off with those shoes: and then safely tread
In this loves hallow'd temple, this soft bed.
In such white robes heavens Angels us'd to bee
Receiv'd by men; Thou Angel bring'st with thee
A heaven like Mahomets Paradise: and though
Ill spirits walk in white, we easily know,
By this these Angels from an evill sprite:
They set our haires, but these the flesh upright.

   Licence my roaving hands, and let them goe
Behind, before, above, between, below.
O my America, my new found lande,
My kingdome, safeliest when with one man man'd,
My myne of precious stones, My Emperee,
How blest am I in this discovering thee.
To enter in these bonds, is to be free,
Then where my hand is set my seal shall be.
   Full nakedness, all joyes are due to thee.
As soules unbodied, bodies uncloth'd must bee
To taste whole joyes. Gems which you women use
Are as Atlanta's balls, cast in mens viewes,
That when a fooles eye lighteth on a gem
His earthly soule may covet theirs not them.
Like pictures, or like bookes gay coverings made
For laymen, are all women thus arraid;
Themselves are mystique books, which only wee
Whom their imputed grace will dignify
Must see reveal'd. Then since that I may knowe,
As liberally as to a midwife showe
Thy selfe: cast all, yea, this white linnen hence,
There is no pennance, much lesse innocence.
   To teach thee, I am naked first: why then
What need'st thou have more covering than a man.

ROGER MCGOUGH 1937–

From SUMMER WITH MONIKA

ten milk bottles standing in the hall
ten milk bottles up against the wall
next door neighbour thinks we're dead
hasnt heard a sound he said
doesn't know weve been in bed
the ten whole days since we were wed

noone knows and noone sees
we lovers doing as we please
but people stop and point at these
ten milk bottles a-turning into cheese

ten milk bottles standing day and night
ten different thicknesses and
different shades of white
persistent carolsingers without a note to utter
silent carolsingers a-turning into butter

now she's run out of passion
and theres not much left in me
so maybe we'll get up
and make a cup of tea
then people can stop wondering
what theyre waiting for
those ten milk bottles a-queuing at our door
those ten milk bottles a-queuing at our door

ELIZABETH BARRETT BROWNING 1806–61

SONNET FROM THE PORTUGUESE XLIII

How do I love thee? Let me count the ways.
I love thee to the depth and breadth and height
My soul can reach, when feeling out of sight
For the ends of Being and ideal Grace.
I love thee to the level of everyday's
Most quiet need, by sun and candlelight.
I love thee freely, as men strive for Right;
I love thee purely, as they turn from Praise.
I love thee with the passion put to use
In my old griefs, and with my childhood's faith.
I love thee with a love I seemed to lose
With my lost saints, – I love thee with the breath,
Smiles, tears, of all my life! – and, if God choose,
I shall but love thee better after death.

EDWARD LEAR 1812–88

THE OWL AND THE PUSSY-CAT

The Owl and the Pussy-Cat went to sea
   In a beautiful pea-green boat.
They took some honey, and plenty of money
   Wrapped up in a five-pound note.
The Owl looked up to the stars above,
   And sang to a small guitar,
'O lovely Pussy! O Pussy, my love,
What a beautiful Pussy you are,
     You are,
     You are!
What a beautiful Pussy you are!'

Pussy said to Owl, 'You elegant fowl!
   How charmingly sweet you sing!
O let us be married! too long we have tarried:
   But what shall we do for a ring?'
They sailed away, for a year and a day,
   To the land where the Bong-Tree grows,
And there in a wood a Piggy-wig stood,
With a ring at the end of his nose,
     His nose,
     His nose!
With a ring at the end of his nose.

'Dear Pig, are you willing to sell for one shilling
   Your ring?' Said the Piggy, 'I will.'
So they took it away, and were married next day
   By the Turkey who lives on the hill.
They dinèd on mince, and slices of quince,
   Which they ate with a runcible spoon;
And hand in hand, on the edge of the sand
   They danced by the light of the moon,
     The moon,
     The moon,
They danced by the light of the moon.

In Warning of Love

A.E. HOUSMAN 1859–1936

WHEN I WAS ONE-AND-TWENTY
from *A Shropshire Lad*

When I was one-and-twenty
 I heard a wise man say,
'Give crowns and pounds and guineas
 But not your heart away;
Give pearls away and rubies
 But keep your fancy free.'
But I was one-and-twenty,
 No use to talk to me.

When I was one-and-twenty
 I heard him say again,
'The heart out of the bosom
 Was never given in vain;
'Tis paid with sighs a plenty
 And sold for endless rue.'
And I am two-and-twenty,
 And oh, 'tis true, 'tis true.

JOHN KEATS 1795–1821

LA BELLE DAME SANS MERCI

O what can ail thee, knight-at-arms,
　　Alone and palely loitering?
The sedge has withered from the lake,
　　　And no birds sing.

O what can ail thee, knight-at-arms,
　　So haggard and so woe-begone?
The squirrel's granary is full,
　　　And the harvest's done.

I see a lilly on thy brow
　　With anguish moist and fever dew;
And on thy cheek a fading rose
　　　Fast withereth too.

I met a lady in the meads,
　　Full beautiful – a faery's child,
Her hair was long, her foot was light,
　　　And her eyes were wild.

I made a garland for her head,
　　And bracelets too, and fragrant zone;
She looked at me as she did love,
　　　And made sweet moan.

I set her on my pacing steed
　　And nothing else saw all day long,
For sideways would she lean, and sing
　　　A faery's song.

She found me roots of relish sweet,
   And honey wild and manna dew,
And sure in language strange she said –
     'I love thee true'.

She took me to her elfin grot
   And there she wept and sigh'd full sore,
And there I shut her wild, wild eyes
     With kisses four.

And there she lulled me asleep,
   And there I dream'd – Ah! woe betide!
The latest dream I ever dream'd
     On the cold hill side.

I saw pale kings and princes too,
   Pale warriors, death-pale were they all;
Who cried – 'La Belle Dame sans Merci
     Hath thee in thrall!'

I saw their starved lips in the gloam
   With horrid warning gaped wide,
And I awoke and found me here
     On the cold hill's side.

And this is why I sojourn here
   Alone and palely loitering,
Though the sedge is withered from the lake,
     And no birds sing.

JENNY JOSEPH 1932–

IN HONOUR OF LOVE

In your honour I have cleaned the windows
Of four-months' sorrow-flung obscuration and dirt
And cut my hair and thrown away old rags
That make cupboards foetid, suffused with miserly pain.
I shall wipe the mould out of the corners
Rub down, prepare to paint;   in your honour.

And in your honour
Am throwing out old nastiness with the floorboards,
Memories of hurt, lese-majesty
Along with the shards and glue, useless and hard now.

As if for new love turning a new leaf over
I will pick off infestation up to the minute.
At this time of budding give a chance to cleanliness
Make beds freshly in garden, and in the house
Fresh covers; as if with hope square corners
In expectation, in honour of your coming.

For your comfort and in your honour
I have laid by stores and funds of robustness
Sweeping despondence out with the spiders' coatings
Disinfecting anxiety, self-pity
The damp that clads, sours and eats the woodwork.

I think it isn't true that ghosts return
Only to ruins and to broken things.
Shy visitants that start to come with me
Along the track I make you from the past
By thinking of you, you would never bear
Burdens you could not shoulder when alive.
You'll still want cheering, self-reliance, comfort
The big wheel pulling up the hill, hearth cleared,
Coal ordered, landlord dealt with; 'sociables',
And so to welcome you and keep a place
For your reviving influence to bide in
I move within the chrysalis of doubt
Wound round for winter comfort, for survival.

In honour of love, in hope of expectation
I leave behind drab covering that kept me
Safe through the winter, safe and solitary.

The grub without its carapace is needed
Pale and soft and vulnerable, for birds
Shining and voracious.   So,
I am persuaded, every time a fool.
Well, something must feed the remorselessness of spring.

The skin will burst, so you should see light wings
No dirty brown slough. The bad times swept away,
Place ready for the prodigal,
                              and be damned the peril
The piercing light and the brief high flight will bring.

Ashes, when you have gone, burnt bits on the lamp
That lit you on your way, but in your honour
As you pass by the window, love, – bright flame.

WILLIAM BLAKE 1757–1827

THE CLOD AND THE PEBBLE

'Love seeketh not itself to please,
Nor for itself hath any care,
But for another gives its ease,
And builds a Heaven in Hell's despair.'

So sung a little Clod of Clay
Trodden with the cattle's feet,
But a pebble of the brook
Warbled out these metres meet:

'Love seeketh only self to please,
To bind another to its delight,
Joys in another's loss of ease,
And builds a Hell in Heaven's despite.'

DOROTHY PARKER 1893–1967

UNFORTUNATE COINCIDENCE

By the time you swear you're his,
　　Shivering and sighing,
And he vows his passion is
　　Infinite, undying –
Lady, make a note of this:
　　One of you is lying.

TED HUGHES 1930–

LOVESONG

He loved her and she loved him
His kisses sucked out her whole past and future or tried to
He had no other appetite
She bit him she gnawed him she sucked
She wanted him complete inside her
Safe and Sure forever and ever
Their little cries fluttered into the curtains

Her eyes wanted nothing to get away
Her looks nailed down his hands his wrists his elbows
He gripped her hard so that life
Should not drag her from that moment
He wanted all future to cease
He wanted to topple with his arms round her
Off that moment's brink and into nothing
Or everlasting or whatever there was
Her embrace was an immense press
To print him into her bones
His smiles were the garrets of a fairy palace
Where the real world would never come
Her smiles were spider bites
So he would lie still till she felt hungry
His words were occupying armies
Her laughs were an assassin's attempts
His looks were bullets daggers of revenge
Her glances were ghosts in the corner with horrible secrets
His whispers were whips and jackboots
Her kisses were lawyers steadily writing
His caresses were the last hooks of a castaway
Her love-tricks were the grinding of locks
And their deep cries crawled over the floors
Like an animal dragging a great trap

His promises were the surgeon's gag
Her promises took the top off his skull
She would get a brooch made of it
His vows pulled out all her sinews
He showed her how to make a love-knot
Her vows put his eyes in formalin
At the back of her secret drawer
Their screams stuck in the wall
Their heads fell apart into sleep like the two halves
Of a lopped melon, but love is hard to stop

In their entwined sleep they exchanged arms and legs
In their dreams their brains took each other hostage

In the morning they wore each other's face

W.B. YEATS 1865–1939

FOR ANNE GREGORY

Never shall a young man,
Thrown into despair
By those great honey-coloured
Ramparts at your ear,
Love you for yourself alone
And not your yellow hair.'

'But I can get a hair-dye
And set such colour there,
Brown, or black, or carrot,
That young men in despair
May love me for myself alone
And not my yellow hair.'

'I heard an old religious man
But yesternight declare
That he had found a text to prove
That only God, my dear,
Could love you for yourself alone
And not your yellow hair.'

EMILY DICKINSON 1830–86

HE FUMBLES AT YOUR SPIRIT

He fumbles at your Spirit
As Players at the Keys
Before they drop full Music on –
He stuns you by degrees –
Prepares your brittle Nature
For the Ethereal Blow
By fainter Hammers – further heard –
Then nearer – Then so slow
Your Breath has time to straighten –
Your Brain – to bubble Cool –
Deals – One – imperial – Thunderbolt –
That scalps your naked Soul –

When Winds take Forests in their Paws
The Universe – is still –

ROBERT GRAVES 1895–1985

SYMPTOMS OF LOVE

Love is a universal migraine,
A bright stain on the vision
Blotting out reason.

Symptoms of true love
Are leanness, jealousy,
Laggard dawns;

Are omens and nightmares –
Listening for a knock,
Waiting for a sign:

For a touch of her fingers
In a darkened room,
For a searching look.

Take courage, lover!
Could you endure such grief
At any hand but hers?

– In Warning of Love –

WILLIAM SHAKESPEARE 1564–1616

SONG

from *Twelfth Night*

O Mistris mine, where are you roming?
O stay and heare, your true loves coming,
    That can sing both high and low.
Trip no further prettie sweeting,
Journeys end in lovers meeting,
     Every wise mans sonne doth know.

What is love, tis not heereafter,
Present mirth, hath present laughter:
    What's to come, is still unsure.
In delay there lies no plentie,
Then come kisse me, sweet and twentie:
     Youths a stuffe will not endure.

ROBERT GRAVES 1895–1985

LOVE WITHOUT HOPE

Love without hope, as when the young bird-catcher
Swept off his tall hat to the Squire's own daughter,
So let the imprisoned larks escape and fly
Singing about her head as she rode by.

Love Lost and Love Remembered

— ◇ —

W.H. AUDEN 1907-73

TWELVE SONGS

IX

Stop all the clocks, cut off the telephone,
Prevent the dog from barking with a juicy bone,
Silence the pianos and with muffled drum
Bring out the coffin, let the mourners come.

Let aeroplanes circle moaning overhead
Scribbling on the sky the message He is Dead,
Put crêpe bows round the white necks of the public doves,
Let the traffic policemen wear black cotton gloves.

He was my North, my South, my East and West,
My working week and my Sunday rest,
My noon, my midnight, my talk, my song;
I thought that love would last for ever: I was wrong.

The stars are not wanted now: put out every one;
Pack up the moon and dismantle the sun;
Pour away the ocean and sweep up the wood.
For nothing now can ever come to any good.

ANON

LADY GREENSLEEVES

Alas, my love, ye do me wrong,
  To cast me off disc'urteously:
And I have loved you so long,
  Delighting in your company.

Greensleeves was all my joy,
  Greensleeves was my delight:
Greensleeves was my heart of gold,
And who but Lady Greensleeves.

I have been ready at your hand,
  To grant what ever you would crave.
I have both waged life and land,
  Your love and good will for to have.

Greensleeves was all my joy, etc.

I bought thee kerchers to thy head,
  That were wrought fine and gallantly:
I kept thee both at board and bed,
  Which cost my purse well favouredly,

I bought thee petticoats of the best,
  The cloth so fine as fine might be:
I gave thee jewels for thy chest,
  And all this cost I spent on thee.

Thy smock of silk, both fair and white,
  With gold embroidered gorgeously:
Thy petticoat of sendal right:
  And thus I bought thee gladly.

Thy girdle of gold so red,
  With pearls bedecked sumptuously:
The like no other lasses had,
  And yet thou wouldst not love me,

Thy purse and eke thy gay guilt knives,
    Thy pincase gallant to the eye:
No better wore the burgess wives,
    And yet thou wouldst not love me.

Thy crimson stockings all of silk,
    With gold all wrought above the knee,
Thy pumps as white as was the milk,
    And yet thou wouldst not love me.

Thy gown was of the grossy green,
    Thy sleeves of satin hanging by:
Which made thee be our harvest Queen,
    And yet thou wouldst not love me.

Thy garters fringed with the gold,
    And silver aglets hanging by,
Which made thee blithe for to behold,
    And yet thou wouldst not love me.

My gayest gelding I thee gave,
    To ride where ever liked thee,
No Lady ever was so brave,
    And yet thou wouldst not love me.

My men were clothed all in green,
    And they did ever wait on thee:
All this was gallant to be seen,
    And yet thou wouldst not love me.

They set thee up, they took thee down,
    They served thee with humility,
Thy foot might not once touch the ground,
    And yet thou wouldst not love me.

For every morning when thou rose,
  I sent thee dainties orderly:
To cheer thy stomach from all woes,
  And yet thou wouldst not love me.

Thou couldst desire no earthly thing.
  But still thou hadst it readily:
Thy music still to play and sing,
  And yet thou wouldst not love me.

And who did pay for all this gear,
  That thou didst spend when pleased,
Even I that am rejected here,
  And thou disdainst to love me.

Well, I will pray to God on high,
  That thou my constancy mayst see:
And that yet once before I die,
  Thou wilt vouchsafe to love me.

Greensleeves now farewell, adieu,
  God I pray to prosper thee:
For I am still thy lover true,
  Come once again and love me.

GEORGE GORDON, LORD BYRON 1788–1824

WHEN WE TWO PARTED

When we two parted
  In silence and tears,
Half broken-hearted,
  To sever for years,
Pale grew thy cheek and cold,
  Colder thy kiss;
Truly that hour foretold
  Sorrow to this.

The dew of the morning
  Sunk chill on my brow –
It felt like the warning
  Of what I feel now.
Thy vows are all broken,
  And light is thy fame;
I hear thy name spoken
  And share in its shame.

They name thee before me,
  A knell to mine ear;
A shudder comes o'er me –
  Why wert thou so dear?
They know not I knew thee,
  Who knew thee too well: –
Long, long shall I rue thee,
  Too deeply to tell.

In secret we met –
  In silence I grieve,
That thy heart could forget,
  Thy spirit deceive.
If I should meet thee
  After long years,
How should I greet thee? –
  With silence and tears.

SIR THOMAS WYATT 1503–42

THEY FLE FROM ME THAT SOMETYME DID ME SEKE

They fle from me that sometyme did me seke
   With naked fote stalking in my chambre.
I have sene theim gentill tame and meke
    That nowe are wyld and do not remembre
    That sometyme they put theimself in daunger
To take bred at my hand; and nowe they raunge
Besely seking with a continuell chaunge.

Thancked be fortune, it hath ben othrewise
   Twenty tymes better; but ons in speciall,
In thyn arraye after a pleasaunt gyse,
    When her lose gowne from her shoulders did fall,
    And she me caught in her armes long and small;
Therewithall swetely did me kysse,
And softely saide, *dere hert, howe like you this?*

It was no dreme: I lay brode waking.
   But all is torned thorough my gentilnes
Into a straunge fasshion of forsaking;
    And I have leve to goo of her goodenes,
    And she also to vse new fangilnes.
But syns that I so kyndely ame serued,
I would fain knowe what she hath deserued.

WILLIAM BLAKE 1757–1827

NEVER SEEK TO TELL THY LOVE

Never seek to tell thy love,
Love that never told can be;
For the gentle wind does move
Silently, invisibly.

I told my love, I told my love.
I told her all my heart,
Trembling, cold, in ghastly fears –
Ah, she doth depart.

Soon as she was gone from me
A traveller came by
Silently, invisibly –
He took her with a sigh. O, was no deny.

EDWARD LEAR 1812–88

THE COURTSHIP OF THE YONGHY-BONGHY-BÒ

On the Coast of Coromandel
  Where the early pumpkins blow,
    In the middle of the woods
  Lived the Yonghy-Bonghy-Bò.
Two old chairs, and half a candle, –
One old jug without a handle, –
    These were all his worldly goods:
    In the middle of the woods,
    These were all the worldly goods,
  Of the Yonghy-Bonghy-Bò,
  Of the Yonghy-Bonghy-Bò.

Once, among the Bong-trees walking
  Where the early pumpkins blow,
    To a little heap of stones
  Came the Yonghy-Bonghy-Bò.
There he heard a Lady talking,
To some milk-white Hens of Dorking, –
    ' 'Tis the Lady Jingly Jones!
    'On that little heap of stones
    'Sits the Lady Jingly Jones!'
  Said the Yonghy-Bonghy-Bò.
  Said the Yonghy-Bonghy-Bò.

'Lady Jingly! Lady Jingly!
  'Sitting where the pumpkins blow,
    'Will you come and be my wife?'
  Said the Yonghy-Bonghy-Bò.
'I am tired of living singly, –
'On this coast so wild and shingly, –
    'I'm a-weary of my life;
    'If you'll come and be my wife,
    'Quite serene would be my life!' –
  Said the Yonghy-Bonghy-Bò,
  Said the Yonghy-Bonghy-Bò.

'On this Coast of Coromandel,
   'Shrimps and watercresses grow,
     'Prawns are plentiful and cheap,'
  Said the Yonghy-Bonghy-Bò.
'You shall have my chairs and candle,
'And my jug without a handle! –
     'Gaze upon the rolling deep
     '(Fish is plentiful and cheap);
     'As the sea, my love is deep!'
  Said the Yonghy-Bonghy-Bò.
  Said the Yonghy-Bonghy-Bò.

Lady Jingly answered sadly,
  And her tears began to flow, –
     'Your proposal comes too late,
  'Mr. Yonghy-Bonghy-Bò!
'I would be your wife most gladly!'
(Here she twirled her fingers madly)
     'But in England I've a mate!
     'Yes! you've asked me far too late,
     'For in England I've a mate,
  'Mr. Yonghy-Bonghy-Bò!
  'Mr. Yonghy-Bonghy-Bò!

'Mr. Jones – (his name is Handel, –
  'Handel Jones, Esquire, & Co.)
     'Dorking fowls delights to send,
  'Mr. Yonghy-Bonghy-Bò!
'Keep, oh! keep your chairs and candle,
'And your jug without a handle, –
     'I can merely be your friend!
     ' – Should my Jones more Dorkings send,
     'I will give you three, my friend!
  'Mr. Yonghy-Bonghy-Bò!
  'Mr. Yonghy-Bonghy-Bò!

'Though you've such a tiny body,
  'And your head so large doth grow, –
    'Though your hat may blow away,
  'Mr. Yonghy-Bonghy-Bò!
'Though you're such a Hoddy Doddy –
'Yet I wish that I could modi-
    'fy the words I needs must say!
    'Will you please to go away?
    'That is all I have to say –
  'Mr. Yonghy-Bonghy-Bò!
  'Mr. Yonghy-Bonghy-Bò!'

Down the slippery slopes of Myrtle,
  Where the early pumpkins blow,
    To the calm and silent sea
  Fled the Yonghy-Bonghy-Bò.
There, beyond the Bay of Gurtle,
Lay a large and lively Turtle; –
    'You're the Cove,' he said, 'for me;
    'On your back beyond the sea,
    'Turtle, you shall carry me!'
Said the Yonghy-Bonghy-Bò,
Said the Yonghy-Bonghy-Bò.

Through the silent-roaring ocean
　　Did the Turtle swiftly go;
　　　Holding fast upon his shell
　　Rode the Yonghy-Bonghy-Bò.
With a sad primaeval motion
Towards the sunset isles of Boshen
　　　Still the Turtle bore him well.
　　　Holding fast upon his shell,
　　　'Lady Jingly Jones, farewell!'
Sang the Yonghy-Bonghy-Bò,
Sang the Yonghy-Bonghy-Bò.

From the Coast of Coromandel,
　　Did that Lady never go;
　　　On that heap of stones she mourns
　　For the Yonghy-Bonghy-Bò.
On the Coast of Coromandel,
In his jug without a handle,
　　　Still she weeps, and daily moans;
　　　On that little heap of stones
　　　To her Dorking Hens she moans,
For the Yonghy-Bonghy-Bò,
For the Yonghy-Bonghy-Bò.

W.B. YEATS 1865–1939

DOWN BY THE SALLEY GARDENS

Down by the salley gardens my love and I did meet;
She passed the salley gardens with little snow-white feet.
She bid me take love easy, as the leaves grow on the tree;
But I, being young and foolish, with her would not agree.

In a field by the river my love and I did stand,
And on my leaning shoulder she laid her snow-white hand.
She bid me take life easy, as the grass grows on the weirs;
But I was young and foolish, and now am full of tears.

JOHN CLARE 1793–1864

THE SECRET

I loved thee, though I told thee not,
　　Right earlily and long,
Thou wert my joy in every spot,
　　My theme in every song.

And when I saw a stranger face
　　Where beauty held the claim,
I gave it like a secret grace
　　The being of thy name.

And all the charms of face or voice
　　Which I in others see
Are but the recollected choice
　　Of what I felt for thee.

THOMAS HARDY 1840–1928

TO LIZBIE BROWNE

I

Dear Lizbie Browne,
Where are you now?
In sun, in rain? –
Or is your brow
Past joy, past pain,
Dear Lizbie Browne?

II

Sweet Lizbie Browne,
How you could smile,
How you could sing! –
How archly wile
In glance-giving,
Sweet Lizbie Browne!

III

And, Lizbie Browne,
Who else had hair
Bay-red as yours,
Or flesh so fair
Bred out of doors,
Sweet Lizbie Browne?

IV

When, Lizbie Browne,
You had just begun
To be endeared
By stealth to one,
You disappeared,
My Lizbie Browne!

V

Ay, Lizbie Browne,
So swift your life,
And mine so slow,
You were a wife
Ere I could show
Love, Lizbie Browne.

VI

Still, Lizbie Browne,
You won, they said,
The best of men
When you were wed . . .
Where went you then,
O Lizbie Browne?

VII

Dear Lizbie Browne,
I should have thought,
'Girls ripen fast,'
And coaxed and caught
You ere you passed,
Dear Lizbie Browne!

VIII

But, Lizbie Browne,
I let you slip;
Shaped not a sign;
Touched never your lip
With lip of mine,
Lost Lizbie Browne!

IX
So, Lizbie Browne,
When on a day
Men speak of me
As not, you'll say,
'And who was he?' –
Yes, Lizbie Browne!
1901

EDWARD THOMAS 1878–1917

'GO NOW'

Like the touch of rain she was
On a man's flesh and hair and eyes
When the joy of walking thus
Has taken him by surprise:

With the love of the storm he burns,
He sings, he laughs, well I know how,
But forgets when he returns
As I shall not forget her 'Go now'.

Those two words shut a door
Between me and the blessed rain
That was never shut before
And will not open again.

MICHAEL DRAYTON 1563–1631

LOVE'S FAREWELL

Since ther's no helpe, come let us kisse and part,
Nay, I have done: you get no more of me,
And I am glad, yea, glad with all my heart,
That thus so cleanly, I my selfe can free,
Shake hands for ever, cancell all our vowes,
And when we meet at any time againe,
Be it not seene in either of our browes,
That we one jot of former love reteyne;
Now at the last gaspe, of love's latest breath,
When his pulse fayling, passion speechlesse lies,
When faith is kneeling by his bed of death,
And innocence is closing up his eyes,

  Now if thou would'st, when all have given him over,
  From death to life thou might'st him yet recover.

THOMAS HARDY 1840–1928

AFTER A JOURNEY

Hereto I come to view a voiceless ghost;
   Whither, O whither will its whim now draw me?
Up the cliff, down, till I'm lonely, lost,
   And the unseen waters' ejaculations awe me.
Where you will next be there's no knowing,
   Facing round about me everywhere,
     With your nut-coloured hair,
And gray eyes, and rose-flush coming and going.

Yes: I have re-entered your olden haunts at last;
   Through the years, through the dead scenes I have tracked you;
What have you now found to say of our past –
   Scanned across the dark space wherein I have lacked you?
Summer gave us sweets, but autumn wrought division?
   Things were not lastly as firstly well
     With us twain, you tell?
But all's closed now, despite Time's derision.

I see what you are doing: you are leading me on
   To the spots we knew when we haunted here together,
The waterfall, above which the mist-bow shone
   At the then fair hour in the then fair weather,
And the cave just under, with a voice still so hollow
   That it seems to call out to me from forty years ago,
     When you were all aglow,
And not the thin ghost that I now fraily follow!

Ignorant of what there is flitting here to see,
   The waked birds preen and the seals flop lazily,
Soon you will have, Dear, to vanish from me,
   For the stars close their shutters and the dawn whitens hazily.
Trust me, I mind not, though Life lours,
   The bringing me here; nay, bring me here again!
     I am just the same as when
Our days were a joy, and our paths through flowers.
                Pentargan Bay

VICKI FEAVER 1943–

COAT

Sometimes I have wanted
to throw you off
like a heavy coat.

Sometimes I have said
you would not let me
breathe or move.

But now that I am free
to choose light clothes
or none at all

I feel the cold
and all the time I think
how warm it used to be.

ELIZABETH BISHOP 1911–79

ONE ART

The art of losing isn't hard to master;
so many things seem filled with the intent
to be lost that their loss is no disaster.

Lose something every day. Accept the fluster
of lost door keys, the hour badly spent.
The art of losing isn't hard to master.

Then practice losing farther, losing faster:
places, and names, and where it was you meant
to travel. None of these will bring disaster.

I lost my mother's watch. And look! my last, or
next-to-last, of three loved houses went.
The art of losing isn't hard to master.

I lost two cities, lovely ones. And, vaster,
some realms I owned, two rivers, a continent.
I miss them, but it wasn't a disaster.

– Even losing you (the joking voice, a gesture
I love) I shan't have lied. It's evident
the art of losing's not too hard to master
though it may look like (*Write* it!) like disaster.

SIR JOHN BETJEMAN 1906–84

INDOOR GAMES NEAR NEWBURY

In among the silver birches winding ways of tarmac wander
  And the signs to Bussock Bottom, Tussock Wood and Windy Brake,
Gabled lodges, tile-hung churches, catch the lights of our Lagonda
  As we drive to Wendy's party, lemon curd and Christmas cake.

Rich the makes of motor whirring, past the pine-plantation purring
  Come up, Hupmobile, Delage!
Short the way your chauffeurs travel, crunching over private gravel
  Each from out his warm garáge.

Oh but Wendy, when the carpet yielded to my indoor pumps
  There you stood, your gold hair streaming, handsome in the hall-light
    gleaming
There you looked and there you led me off into the game of clumps
  Then the new Victrola playing and your funny uncle saying
'Choose your partners for a fox-trot! Dance until its *tea* o'clock!
  'Come on, young 'uns, foot it featly!' Was it chance that paired us
    neatly,
  I, who loved you so completely,
You, who pressed me closely to you, hard against your party frock!

'Meet me when you've finished eating!' So we met and no one found us.
   Oh that dark and furry cupboard while the rest played hide and seek!
Holding hands our two hearts beating in the bedroom silence round us,
   Holding hands and hardly hearing sudden footstep, thud and shriek.
Love that lay too deep for kissing – 'Where *is* Wendy? Wendy's missing!'
      Love so pure it *had* to end,
Love so strong that I was frighten'd when you gripped
   my fingers tight and
      Hugging, whispered 'I'm your friend.'

Good-bye Wendy! Send the fairies, pinewood elf and larch tree gnome,
   Spingle-spangled stars are peeping at the lush Lagonda creeping
Down the winding ways of tarmac to the leaded lights of home.
   There, among the silver birches, all the bells of all the churches
Sounded in the bath-waste running out into the frosty air.
   Wendy speeded my undressing, Wendy is the sheet's caressing
      Wendy bending gives a blessing,
Holds me as I drift to dreamland, safe inside my slumber wear.

ERNEST DOWSON 1867–1900

NON SUM QUALIS ERAM BONAE
SUB REGNO CYNARAE

Last night, ah, yesternight, betwixt her lips and mine
There fell thy shadow, Cynara! thy breath was shed
Upon my soul between the kisses and the wine;
And I was desolate and sick of an old passion,
    Yea, I was desolate and bowed my head:
I have been faithful to thee, Cynara! in my fashion.

All night upon mine heart I felt her warm heart beat,
Night-long within mine arms in love and sleep she lay;
Surely the kisses of her bought red mouth were sweet;
But I was desolate and sick of an old passion,
    When I awoke and found the dawn was gray:
I have been faithful to thee, Cynara! in my fashion.

I have forgot much, Cynara! gone with the wind,
Flung roses, roses riotously with the throng,
Dancing, to put thy pale, lost lilies out of mind;
But I was desolate and sick of an old passion,
    Yea, all the time, because the dance was long:
I have been faithful to thee, Cynara! in my fashion.

I cried for madder music and for stronger wine,
But when the feast is finished and the lamps expire,
Then falls thy shadow, Cynara! the night is thine;
And I am desolate and sick of an old passion,
    Yea hungry for the lips of my desire:
I have been faithful to thee, Cynara! in my fashion.

A.E. HOUSMAN 1859–1936

OH, WHEN I WAS IN LOVE WITH YOU
from *A Shropshire Lad*

Oh, when I was in love with you,
  Then I was clean and brave,
And miles around the wonder grew
  How well did I behave.

And now the fancy passes by,
  And nothing will remain,
And miles around they'll say that I
  Am quite myself again.

RUPERT BROOKE 1887–1915

THE HILL

Breathless, we flung us on the windy hill,
    Laughed in the sun, and kissed the lovely grass.
    You said, 'Through glory and ecstasy we pass;
Wind, sun, and earth remain, the birds sing still,
When we are old, are old . . .' 'And when we die
All's over that is ours; and life burns on
Through other lovers, other lips,' said I,
'Heart of my heart, our heaven is now, is won!'

'We are Earth's best, that learnt her lesson here.
    Life is our cry. We have kept the faith!' we said;
    'We shall go down with unreluctant tread
Rose-crowned into the darkness!'. . . Proud we were,
And laughed, that had such brave true things to say.
– And then you suddenly cried, and turned away.
                                                    1910

ROBERT BROWNING 1812–89

LOVE IN A LIFE

Room after room,
I hunt the house through
We inhabit together.
Heart, fear nothing, for, heart, thou shalt find her –
Next time, herself! – not the trouble behind her
Left in the curtain, the couch's perfume!
As she brushed it, the cornice-wreath blossomed anew:
Yon looking-glass gleamed at the wave of her feather.

Yet the day wears,
And door succeeds door;
I try the fresh fortune –
Range the wide house from the wing to the centre.
Still the same chance! she goes out as I enter.
Spend my whole day in the quest, – who cares?
But 'tis   twilight, you see, – with such suites to explore,
Such closets to search, such alcoves to importune!

EMILY BRONTE 1818–48

R. ALCONA TO J. BRENZAIDA

Cold in the earth, and the deep snow piled above thee!
Far, far removed, cold in the dreary grave!
Have I forgot, my Only Love, to love thee,
Severed at last by Time's all-wearing wave?

Now, when alone, do my thoughts no longer hover
Over the mountains on Angora's shore;
Resting their wings where heath and fern-leaves cover
That noble heart for ever, ever more?

Cold in the earth, and fifteen wild Decembers
From those brown hills have melted into spring –
Faithful indeed is the spirit that remembers
After such years of change and suffering!

Sweet Love of youth, forgive if I forget thee
While the World's tide is bearing me along:
Sterner desires and darker hopes beset me,
Hopes which obscure but cannot do thee wrong.

No other Sun has lightened up my heaven;
No other Star has ever shone for me:
All my life's bliss from thy dear life was given –
All my life's bliss is in the grave with thee.

But when the days of golden dreams had perished
And even Despair was powerless to destroy,
Then did I learn how existence could be cherished,
Strengthened and fed without the aid of joy;

Then did I check the tears of useless passion,
Weaned my young soul from yearning after thine;
Sternly denied its burning wish to hasten
Down to that tomb already more than mine!

And even yet, I dare not let it languish,
Dare not indulge in Memory's rapturous pain;
Once drinking deep of that divinest anguish,
How could I seek the empty world again?

ALICE MEYNELL 1847–1922

RENOUNCEMENT

I must not think of thee; and, tired yet strong,
   I shun the thought that lurks in all delight –
   The thought of thee – and in the blue Heaven's height,
And in the sweetest passage of a song.
O just beyond the fairest thoughts that throng
   This breast, the thought of thee waits hidden yet bright;
   But it must never, never come in sight;
I must stop short of thee the whole day long.
But when sleep comes to close each difficult day,
   When night gives pause to the long watch I keep,
     And all my bonds I needs must loose apart,
Must doff my will as raiment laid away, –
   With the first dream that comes with the first sleep
     I run, I run, I am gathered to thy heart.

THOMAS HARDY 1840–1928

THE VOICE

Woman much missed, how you call to me, call to me,
Saying that now you are not as you were
When you had changed from the one who was all to me,
But as at first, when our day was fair.

Can it be you that I hear? Let me view you, then,
Standing as when I drew near to the town
Where you would wait for me: yes, as I knew you then,
Even to the original air-blue gown!

Or is it only the breeze, in its listlessness
Travelling across the wet mead to me here,
You being ever dissolved to wan wistlessness,
Heard no more again far or near?

   Thus I; faltering forward,
   Leaves around me falling,
Wind oozing thin through the thorn from norward,
   And the woman calling.

December 1912

EDNA ST. VINCENT MILLAY 1892–1950

SONNET II

Time does not bring relief; you all have lied
Who told me time would ease me of my pain!
I miss him in the weeping of the rain;
I want him at the shrinking of the tide;
The old snows melt from every mountain-side,
And last year's leaves are smoke in every lane;
But last year's bitter loving must remain
Heaped on my heart, and my old thoughts abide!
There are a hundred places where I fear
To go, – so with his memory they brim!
And entering with relief some quiet place
Where never fell his foot or shone his face
I say, 'There is no memory of him here!'
And so stand stricken, so remembering him.

PHILIP LARKIN 1922–85

LOVE SONGS IN AGE

She kept her songs, they took so little space,
    The covers pleased her:
One bleached from lying in a sunny place,
One marked in circles by a vase of water,
One mended, when a tidy fit had seized her,
    And coloured, by her daughter –
So they had waited, till in widowhood
She found them, looking for something else, and stood

Relearning how each frank submissive chord
    Had ushered in
Word after sprawling hyphenated word,
And the unfailing sense of being young
Spread out like a spring-woken tree, wherein
    That hidden freshness sung,
That certainty of time laid up in store
As when she played them first. But, even more,

The glare of that much-mentioned brilliance, love,
    Broke out, to show
Its bright incipience sailing above,
Still promising to solve, and satisfy,
And set unchangeably in order. So
    To pile them back, to cry,
Was hard, without lamely admitting how
It had not done so then, and could not now.
            1 January 1957

WILLIAM WORDSWORTH 1770–1850

THE LOST LOVE

She dwelt among the untrodden ways
   Beside the springs of Dove;
A Maid whom there were none to praise
   And very few to love:

A violet by a mossy stone
   Half-hidden from the eye!
– Fair as a star, when only one
   Is shining in the sky.

She lived unknown, and few could know
   When Lucy ceased to be;
But she is in her grave, and, oh,
   The difference to me!

GEORGE GORDON, LORD BYRON 1788–1824

SO, WE'LL GO NO MORE A-ROVING

So, we'll go no more a-roving
　So late into the night,
Though the heart be still as loving,
　And the moon be still as bright.

For the sword outwears its sheath,
　And the soul wears out the breast,
And the heart must pause to breathe,
　And love itself have rest.

Though the night was made for loving,
　And the day returns too soon,
Yet we'll go no more a-roving
　　By the light of the moon.

– Love Lost and Love Remembered –

HILLAIRE BELLOC 1870–1953

TARANTELLA

Do you remember an Inn,
Miranda?
Do you remember an Inn?
And the tedding and the spreading
Of the straw for a bedding,
And the fleas that tease in the High Pyrenees,
And the wine that tasted of the tar?
And the cheers and the jeers of the young muleteers
(Under the vine of the dark verandah)?
Do you remember an Inn, Miranda,
Do you remember an Inn?
And the cheers and the jeers of the young muleteers
Who hadn't got a penny,
And who weren't paying any,
And the hammer at the doors and the Din?
And the Hip! Hop! Hap!
Of the clap
Of the hands to the twirl and the swirl
Of the girl gone chancing,
Glancing,
Dancing,
Backing and advancing,
Snapping of a clapper to the spin
Out and in –
And the Ting, Tong, Tang of the Guitar!
Do you remember an Inn,
Miranda?
Do you remember an Inn!

Never more;
Miranda,
Never more.
Only the high peaks hoar:
And Aragon a torrent at the door.
No sound
In the walls of the Halls where falls
The tread
Of the feet of the dead to the ground
No sound:
But the boom
Of the far Waterfall like Doom.

LEIGH HUNT 1784–1859

JENNY KISSED ME

Jenny kiss'd me when we met,
   Jumping from the chair she sat in;
Time, you thief, who love to get
   Sweets into your list, put that in!
Say I'm weary, say I'm sad,
   Say that health and wealth have miss'd me,
Say I'm growing old, but add,
   Jenny kiss'd me.

W.B. YEATS 1865–1939

WHEN YOU ARE OLD

When you are old and grey and full of sleep,
And nodding by the fire, take down this book,
And slowly read, and dream of the soft look
Your eyes had once, and of their shadows deep;

How many loved your moments of glad grace,
And loved your beauty with love false or true,
But one man loved the pilgrim soul in you,
And loved the sorrows of your changing face;

And bending down beside the glowing bars,
Murmur, a little sadly, how Love fled
And paced upon the mountains overhead
And hid his face amid a crowd of stars.

ACKNOWLEDGEMENTS

— ❖ —

The publishers would like to acknowledge the following for permission to reproduce copyright material.

17, 104, 122, 149. A.P. Watt Ltd on behalf of Michael Yeats for 'He Wishes for the Cloths of Heaven', 'For Anne Gregory', 'Down by the Salley Gardens' and 'When you are old' from *The Collected Poems* of W.B. Yeats.

18, 78, 111. Faber and Faber Ltd for 'Some Say that Love's a Little Boy', 'Lullaby' and 'Stop all the Clocks, cut off the telephone' from 'Twelve Songs' by W.H. Auden from his *Collected Poems*.

23, 28, 48. Faber and Faber Ltd for 'After the Lunch', 'Valentine' and 'Flowers' from *Serious Concerns* by Wendy Cope.

30, 85, 132. John Murray (Publishers) Ltd for 'A Subaltern's Love Song', 'In a Bath Teashop' and 'Indoor Games near Newbury' by Sir John Betjeman from his *Collected Poems*.

41. Faber and Faber Ltd for 'Giving up Smoking' from *Making Cocoa for Kingsley Amis* by Wendy Cope.

46. 'Dea ex machina' (pp 321–322) from *John Updike: Collected Poems 1953–1993* (Hamish Hamilton, 1993) copyright © John Updike, 1985, 1993. Reproduced by permission of Penguin Books Ltd.

50. Faber and Faber Ltd for 'Field Work' from *Field Work* by Seamus Heaney.

52. 'Warming her Pearls' is taken from *Selling Manhattan* by Carol Ann Duffy published by Anvil Press Poetry in 1987.

54. Faber and Faber Ltd for 'You're' from *Ariel* by Sylvia Plath.

56. 'Valentine' from *Collected Poems* by John Fuller. Reprinted by permission of the Peters, Fraser and Dunlop Group Ltd.

59. Faber and Faber Ltd for 'The Confirmation' from *Collected Poems* by Edwin Muir.

60. 'Celia, Celia' from *For Beauty Douglas*. Reprinted by permission of The Peters Fraser and Dunlop Group Limited on behalf of Adrian Mitchell. Adrian Mitchell asks that none of his poems are used in connection with any examinations whatsoever. © Adrian Mitchell.

65. 'Words, Wide Night' is taken from *The Other Country* by Carol Ann Duffy published by Anvil Press Poetry in 1990.

75. Words from *The Prophet* by Kahlil Gibran are used by permission from The National Committee of Gibran 1951. © all rights reserved.

86. 'Wedding Wind' by Philip Larkin is reprinted from *The Less Deceived* by permission of The Marvell Press, England and Australia.

90. Part 2 ('Ten Milk Bottles') of *Summer with Monika* by Roger McGough. Reprinted by permission of The Peters Fraser and Dunlop Group Limited on behalf of Roger McGough © Roger McGough.

95, 135. The Society of Authors as the literary representative of the Estate of A.E. Housman for 'When I was one-and-twenty' and 'Oh, when I was in love with you' from *A Shropshire Lad* by A. E. Housman.

98. 'In honour of love' by Jenny Joseph from *Ghosts and Other Company*, published by Bloodaxe, 1995.

101. 'Unfortunate Coincidence' by Dorothy Parker from *Collected Dorothy Parker* by permission of Gerald Duckworth and Co. Ltd.

102. Faber and Faber Ltd for 'Love song' from *Crow* by Ted Hughes.

106, 108. 'Symptoms of Love' and 'Love without Hope' from *Complete Poems* by Robert Graves (1995), reproduced by permission of Carcanet Press Ltd.

124, 129, 141. 'To Lizbie Brown', 'After a Journey' and 'The Voice' from *The Complete Poems* by Thomas Hardy, edited by James Gibson, published by Papermac.

130. 'Coat' by permission of Vicki Feaver.

131. 'One Art' from *The Complete Poems* 1927–1979 by Elizabeth Bishop © 1979, 1983 by Alice Methfessel. Reprinted by permission of Farrar, Strauss and Giroux, Inc.

142. 'Time does not bring Relief' by Edna St. Vincent Millay. From *Collected Poems*, HarperCollins. Copyright 1912, 1923, 1940, 1951 by Edna St. Vincent Millay and Norma Millay Ellis. Reprinted by permission of Elizabeth Barnett, literary executor.

143. Faber and Faber Ltd for 'Love Songs in Age' from *Collected Poems* by Philip Larkin.

146. 'Tarantella' from *Complete Verse* by Hilaire Belloc. Reprinted by permission of The Peters Fraser and Dunlop Group Limited on behalf of The Estate of Hilaire Belloc. © Estate of Hilaire Belloc.

Every effort has been made to trace copyright holders, but in some cases this has not been possible. The publishers would be grateful to hear from any copyright holders not here acknowledged.

INDEX OF POETS' NAMES

— ◇ —

INDEX OF FIRST LINES

— ✧ —

I

J

L

M

N